Need to Know
Allergies

Steve Parker

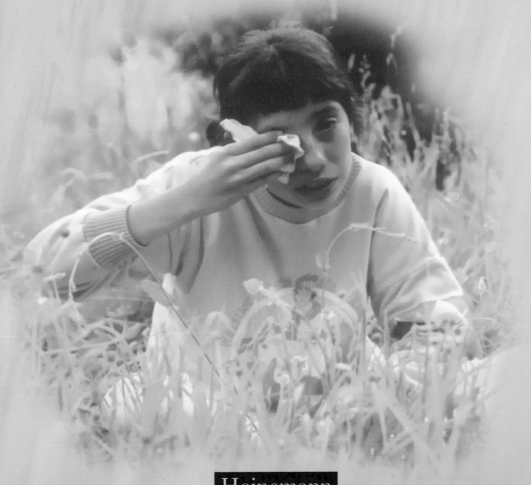

Heinemann
LIBRARY

www.heinemann.co.uk/library
Visit our website to find out more information about **Heinemann Library** books.

To order:
 Phone 44 (0) 1865 888066
 Send a fax to 44 (0) 1865 314091
 Visit the Heinemann Bookshop at www.heinemann.co.uk/library to browse our catalogue and order online.

Produced by Monkey Puzzle Media Ltd
Gissing's Farm, Fressingfield, Suffolk IP21 5SH, UK

First published in Great Britain by Heinemann Library, Halley Court, Jordan Hill, Oxford OX2 8EJ, part of Harcourt Education.
Heinemann is a registered trademark of Harcourt Education Ltd.

Editorial: Katie Orchard
Design: Jane Hawkins
Picture Research: Sally Cole
Consultant: Maureen Jenkins, allergy nurse consultant, Sussex Allergy Services
Production: Viv Hichens

Originated by Ambassador Litho Ltd
Printed and bound in Hong Kong, China by South China Printing Company

ISBN 0 431 09760 7
08 07 06 05 04
10 9 8 7 6 5 4 3 2 1

British Library Cataloguing in Publication Data
Parker, Steve
Allergies – (Need to know)
616.9'7
A full catalogue record for this book is available from the British Library.

Acknowledgements
The publishers would like to thank the following for permission to reproduce photographs:
AKG London p. 6 (Musée Condé); Alamy pp. 15 (David Kamm), 35 (Bob Jones Photography), 36 (Rob Crandell/Stock Connection Inc.); Corbis pp. 30 (Philip Bailey), 49 (Walter Smith); ImageState p. 23 (First Light); MPM Images pp. 27, 39, 43; Press Association p. 26 (EPA); Rex Features pp. 31 (Organic Picture Library), 38 (Phanie Agency); Science Photo Library pp. 1 (John Durham), 5 (David Scharf), 10, 11 (Dr. P. Marazzi), 13 (Susumu Nishinaga), 21 (Eye of Science), 22 (John Durham), 24 (Dr. P. Marazzi), 25 (Jim Selby), 28 (Jerrican Gaillard), 33 (BSIP Astier), 41 (CC Studio), 42 (Jerrican Gaillard), 45 (Josh Sher), 46 (Mark Thomas), 50 (James King-Holmes); Still Pictures p. 19 (Hartmut Schwarzbach); Topham Picturepoint pp. 4 (Rebecca Naden/PA), 16 (Bill Lai/ImageWorks), 18 (Journal-Courier/Steve Warmowski/ ImageWorks); Wellcome Photo Library pp. 7, 8. Cover photographs reproduced courtesy of Science Photo Library/Saturn Stills and Science Photo Library/Conor Caffrey.

Every effort has been made to contact copyright holders of any material reproduced in this book. Any omissions will be rectified in subsequent printings if notice is given to the publishers.
The case studies in this book are based on factual examples. However, in some cases the names or other personal information have been changed to protect the privacy of the individuals concerned.

Contents

Any words appearing in the text in bold, **like this**, are explained in the Glossary.

Allergies

Most people know someone who suffers from an allergy – allergies are very, very widespread. In countries such as the UK, USA and Australia, about one adult in four has an allergy of some kind. Around the world, there are probably more than half a billion (500 million) people who suffer from allergies. They endure irritation, discomfort, pain, limits on daily life, and, in very severe cases, disability.

For some people an **allergic reaction** may last only a few minutes, every now and then. For others it affects them all the time, every day. For a few people, a serious allergy can even be a threat to life itself.

❝Don't forget the pollen [from the grass on the golf course]. I have allergies like a lot of other people ... the stress of competing under those conditions in that environment definitely wears on your immune system.❞

(Tiger Woods [pictured right], US golfing champion, speaking about his hay fever, 2002)

4

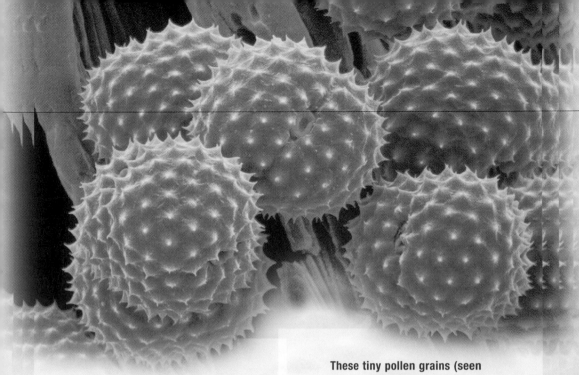

What is an allergy?

The term 'allergy' means different things to different people. For doctors, the word 'allergy' refers to a precise medical condition. But in daily life, the word 'allergy' is often used in a much looser and more casual way. Coughs, colds, wheezes, skin spots, rashes, aches, pains, digestive upsets and even over-excited behaviour are often blamed on 'an allergy'. In some cases this is true. But in many others, the trouble is caused by germs, a small injury, stress, chemicals in food or some other problem. The huge variation in allergic conditions, added to the variety of ways that people use the word 'allergy', causes much confusion about this group of health problems. This book aims to show what an allergy really is, who it affects and how it can be treated.

These tiny pollen grains (seen here under a microscope) may look harmless, but for some people they can trigger the irritating allergy known as hay fever.

Common allergic conditions

Some of the most common conditions are listed below:

- asthma
- allergic rhinitis or hay fever
- perennial rhinitis, such as house-dust mite allergy
- eczema and dermatitis
- urticaria or hives
- food allergies
- allergy to venoms or poisons, such as wasp or bee stings
- allergy to drugs or medications.

These allergies are explained on pages 20–31.

History of allergies

Today, scientists understand that an **allergic reaction** happens when the body's natural defence system, called the **immune system**, tries to fight off a substance that is normally harmless. The immune system usually targets invading **microbes** – germs such as bacteria and viruses. But in a person who has an allergy, the body's defences fight off harmless substances in the same way.

People throughout history have probably suffered from allergies. However, an allergy can often be mistaken for another health problem, such as a cough, cold, skin infection or digestive upset. So allergies may have been occurring, without people realizing, for centuries.

Smelling flowers

One of the most common allergic reactions is to tiny particles called pollen, which plants such as flowers, grasses and trees release into the air. This form of allergy is generally known as hay fever or seasonal allergic **rhinitis**. It causes itchy and watering eyes, an itchy and runny nose, an irritated throat, sneezing and coughing. In 1565 an Italian doctor, Leonardo Botallo, wrote one of the first medical descriptions of hay fever. Botallo described healthy people who, after smelling certain flowers, suffered a runny nose and 'explosive' sneezing.

People through the ages suffered sneezing and wheezing at harvest time, but did not realize it was due to allergy.

Summer catarrh

In 1819 British physician John Bostock wrote a medical report on hay fever – he suffered from it himself. Bostock named it 'summer catarrh' since it resembled a common cold, which produced catarrh (**mucus** and phlegm, slimy fluids produced by the body), but it happened in summer when colds were rare.

In 1831 another English doctor, John Elliotson, wrote a further report on 'summer catarrh'. One of his patients suggested that it seemed to be due to 'an emanation of [something coming from] grass'. This was the first mention of a substance from outside the body being the cause. Elliotson followed up the idea and people began to look for other substances that caused similar problems.

The first allergy tests

In 1880 British physician and researcher, Charles Blackley, wrote one of the first thorough medical books on allergy: *Hay Fever – Its Causes, Treatment and Effective Prevention*. He carried out tests by putting a watery mixture of pollen grains into the eyes of sufferers. Not surprisingly, their eyes became very red, itchy and swollen. At Harvard University in the USA, Morrill Wyman performed similar tests. But exactly why the body reacted in this way was still unknown.

John Elliotson (1791–1868) of University College, London, worked on a wide range of subjects, from allergies to hypnotism.

Allergy breakthroughs

About a century ago scientists began to understand how the body of someone with an allergy reacts. In 1907 an Austrian doctor, Clemens Peter von Pirquet, was researching the serious disease of **tuberculosis** (TB), when he devised the tuberculin skin test. This involved jabbing tuberculin, a substance obtained from the tuberculosis germ, into the skin. If the skin reacted with a red patch or **inflammation**, it showed that the person had

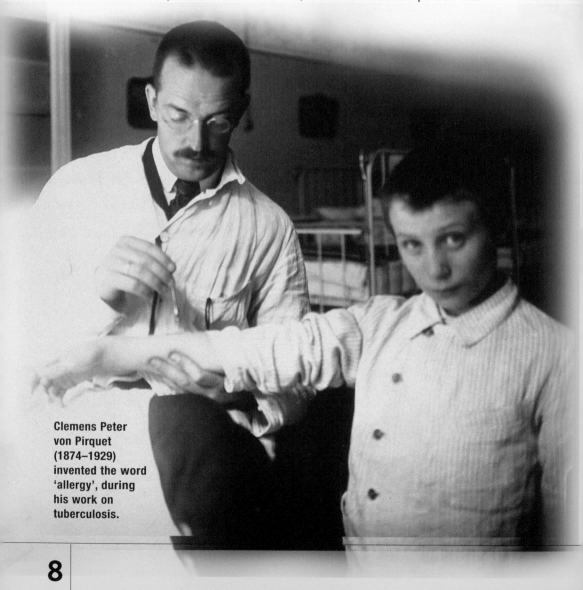

Clemens Peter von Pirquet (1874–1929) invented the word 'allergy', during his work on tuberculosis.

some resistance to the disease. Pirquet also noticed that some people reacted differently to this skin test. He invented a new term for this reaction – allergy, from two ancient Greek words, *allos* meaning 'changed' or 'different', and *ergos* meaning 'action' or 'working'.

The tuberculin skin test was adapted to test people for allergies. Jabbing substances extracted (obtained) from pollen into the skin caused a red, swollen, itchy lump – but only in hay fever sufferers. These people were found to be 'sensitive' or 'allergic' to pollen. Physician Leonard Noon began standard medical tests for sensitivity to pollen in 1911, at St Mary's Hospital, London, UK. Similar types of tests are still used today.

Histamine

From 1904 in London, British scientist Henry Dale studied the substance ergot. This was obtained from a mould that grows on the cereal crop, rye. If people ate foods made from mouldy rye, they suffered various effects due to the ergot, such as spasm or contraction of muscles, paralysis, sudden changes in blood pressure and collapse. Dale wanted to find out if ergot contained chemicals which, in pure form, might be used as helpful medical drugs. In 1910 he purified one chemical, which today is called **histamine**. Dale noticed that if histamine was injected into volunteers, it caused symptoms similar to those of allergies such as **asthma** and hay fever.

Many other scientists became interested in histamine. In 1932 medical scientists Wilhelm Feldberg in Berlin, Germany, and Carl Dragstedt in Chicago, USA, showed that histamine was produced naturally by the body, as tiny granules inside certain microscopic cells, rather than histamine coming from outside the body. When these cells released their histamine in response to a **trigger** such as pollen, the allergic reaction occurred. In the late 1940s research into antihistamine drugs to prevent histamine release began. By the 1950s these drugs were available, but many caused sleepiness or drowsiness. From the 1970s, improved antihistamines appeared, which caused little or no drowsiness in most sufferers.

What is an allergy?

Allergies produce many different symptoms, from red eyes or itchy skin, to coughing and wheezing, violent sickness or sudden collapse. However, these are all caused by the same basic process, the **allergic reaction**. The differences between symptoms depend on where in the body the allergic reaction happens, and how severe it is.

The main type of microscopic body cells involved in allergies are mast cells, which contain histamine, shown here as green specks.

The allergic reaction

An allergic reaction is carried out by the body's **immune system**. Normally, the immune system protects the body against germs and other harmful substances. But in the case of a person with an allergy, the immune system fights against a substance that is normally harmless. The substance that causes or **triggers** the allergic reaction is known as the **allergen**.

Allergens cause the immune system to react by making its own substances to 'fight' them. These are called **antibodies**.

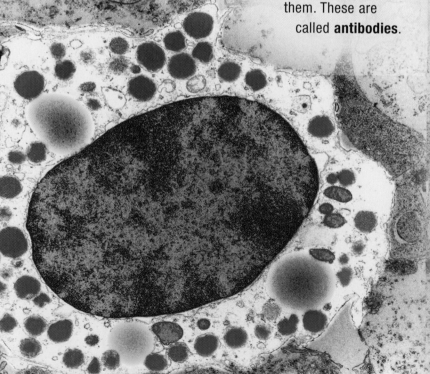

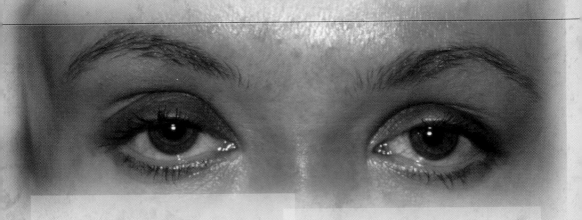

In the body, the antibodies stick to the allergens to damage them, as though they were germs. The antibodies also coat the surfaces of some other cells in the body, known as **mast cells**. These are spread through most of the body, but they are especially numerous near blood vessels, in the skin, and in the linings of the airways, lungs, stomach and intestines. When allergens stick to mast cells, the cells burst open and release a chemical called **histamine** (see page 9). Each mast cell releases about 1,000 tiny particles of histamine.

Histamine causes increased blood flow to the area and attracts various germ-fighting cells and fluids. This is part of the body's normal reaction against disease or injury. The effects are seen as **inflammation** – redness, soreness and swelling due to fluid build-up. However, in an allergy, there is no danger from germs.

In hay fever the allergic reaction affects the delicate surface of the eye (the conjunctiva), making it red, itchy and watery.

The production of antibodies against allergens, the release of histamine from mast cells, and the inflammation and other effects of histamine, are all known as the allergic reaction.

Sensitization

For various reasons (see pages 16–17) some people are more likely than others to develop an allergy. But the allergic reaction does not happen the first time a person encounters the allergen. After this first exposure, the person's immune system 'learns' to recognize the allergen. This can take several days or weeks, and is known as **sensitization**. After the period of sensitization, the allergic reaction happens each time the sufferer comes into contact with the allergen.

What is an allergy?

Types of allergen

Allergies are caused by exposure to allergens – and there are thousands of possible allergens. Some people are allergic to just one or two, while others are allergic to many different kinds. The list includes natural substances such as plant pollen, tiny flakes of animal skin, fur or bird feathers (called **dander**), tiny spores from moulds and fungi, and powdery droppings from minute creatures called **dust mites**. Many modern artificial products and chemicals can cause allergies or allergy-like reactions. These are found in dyes, clothes, cosmetics, detergents, foods, food additives, industrial cleaners, soaps and washing powder, certain medical drugs and metal products. The list grows longer each year.

Targeting different areas

Allergens come into contact with the body in many different ways. Some touch an outer part such as the skin or eyes, or are breathed into the nose, throat and lungs. Others may be eaten and reach the stomach and digestive system, or they may be injected into the body in the form of medication. The way that the allergen makes contact with the body affects the symptoms. For example, in hay fever (seasonal **rhinitis**), floating pollen grains in the air land on the sensitive covering of the eye, and on the moist inner linings of the nose and throat as they are breathed in. So these are the areas that suffer the main allergic reaction.

Allergic reactions tend to happen in **mucus** membranes. These are thin, moist, delicate layers that form the outer coverings or inner linings of many body parts – the nose, throat, airways, lungs, stomach and intestines.

A frightening meal

Neil Drummond, aged 18, lives in London, UK. Neil first discovered that he had a food allergy when he was eight, on a family holiday to the south of France. One evening in a restaurant they ordered *bouillabaisse*, a type of seafood stew. Neil took a few sips of *bouillabaisse*, but decided he did not like it. Within a few minutes, he had itchy red blotches on his skin, and his neck and chin were swollen. He soon felt better but his parents guessed he might be allergic to seafood, so they avoided it for the rest of the holiday. Back at home, Neil went to the doctor and tests showed he was allergic to shellfish.

This is a magnified photo of the lining of the inside of the nose. The 'hairs' are cilia, designed to trap tiny bits of dust and germs – but they also trap pollen grains, which cause hay fever.

A deadly reaction

Anaphylaxis

Sometimes, in rare cases, an **allergic reaction** can be life threatening. It starts at the site affected by the **allergen**, but it gathers speed and severity, spreading through the body in minutes, causing skin rash, redness, itching and swelling. This condition is known as **anaphylaxis** (from the Greek words *ana* and *phulaxis*, meaning 'over-protection'). Accumulation of fluid is noticeable around the face, hands and feet, which look puffy. Fluid also gathers in the airways and lungs, which may become tighter, affecting a person's breathing. The victim may feel weak with a headache, digestive pains, heart flutters and a sense of panic. He or she may faint or collapse as the body's blood pressure falls. If they are not treated in time, they may even die.

Who is at risk?

In countries such as Australia, the USA and the UK, anaphylaxis is the reason for about one in every 500 visits to an emergency medical centre. It is difficult to predict if an allergic reaction will develop into anaphylaxis.

However, if a person has suffered from anaphylaxis before, then it is more likely to occur when exposure happens again to the same allergen.

Almost any type of allergy can lead to anaphylaxis. However, most cases involve food allergies, especially to nuts – for example, peanuts, Brazil nuts, walnuts and almonds (this includes some nut oils as well). Other food culprits are shellfish such as prawns and oysters, fish, sesame seeds, eggs, milk and dairy produce. Anaphylaxis may also occur with allergies to wasp or bee venom, or to drugs such as **antibiotics**. (All of these allergies are discussed in detail on pages 26–31.)

Every second counts

Anaphylaxis is a medical emergency. Seconds count. The vital treatment is an injection of a substance called adrenaline, which reverses the life-threatening effects in the body, plus other drugs. Even if a person recovers from apparent anaphylaxis without treatment, he or she should see a doctor for a medical check-up.

Emergency!

Someone suffering from anaphylaxis needs first aid from an expert, who will follow the procedure below:

1 HELP They will summon emergency help such as an ambulance or paramedic by the quickest means, usually telephone.

2 BREATHING The first-aid expert will put the person in whichever position breathing is easiest, usually lying with legs raised.

3 INFORMATION The expert can ask a conscious victim if he or she has had anaphylaxis before, and what should be done.

4 MEDICATION The expert will check the patient for medication. Some at-risk people carry their own medication, such as tablets or a ready-loaded pen-type injection syringe, or they have a card, bracelet, necklace or other item with an emergency phone number to call.

Who is affected?

The reasons why only some people develop allergies are not well understood. It is not possible to predict if or when a person will develop an allergy. However, there are various factors that make certain groups of people more likely to develop them.

Family history

Allergies are said to 'run in families'. Several people in a family may have the same allergy, such as hay fever, or they may have different allergies. This suggests that they have inherited

genes from their parents that made them more likely than other people to develop an allergy. This is called an inherited 'susceptibility' or 'predisposition' to allergy. However, the numbers of genes and exactly what they do are not yet understood. Also, having these genes does not mean that a person will definitely develop an allergy. In general the chances of developing an allergy are higher for:

- a person whose close family members suffer from allergies;
- a boy rather than a girl;
- a person from a small family of one or two children, rather than a larger family;
- a person whose mother smoked or did not eat healthily during pregnancy.

Early life

Home surroundings during the first months and years of life can affect a person's chances of developing an allergy. However, the reasons why are

Babies who are bottlefed rather than breastfed may be slightly more likely to develop an allergy. But the chances are very small.

not well understood. The chances can be higher for a child who grows up in a house where people smoke, or for a baby who is fed from the bottle (with milk substitutes) rather than breastfed. Changing from baby milk to solid foods relatively early makes it slightly more likely for a child to develop an allergy, as does living in an area with polluted air, or going to a nursery or pre-school day-care centre from a young age. But even if all of these conditions apply to a certain person, this still does not mean that he or she will definitely develop an allergy – it simply increases the likelihood.

Allergies and age

More young children have allergies than older children and adults. In some countries such as the UK and the USA, almost half of babies and children with allergies such as **eczema** or hay fever have 'grown out of them' by the age of 25. Also, the later in life an allergy develops, the more likely it is to last for many years, rather than fade away after a few years. But it is difficult to predict any individual case.

Who is affected?

A growing problem

Allergies are becoming more common. In the past 20 years in industrialized countries such as the UK, USA and Australia, the numbers of allergy sufferers have increased by three or even four times. It is estimated that one person in three under the age of 18 has some form of allergy.

Some aspects of early life can decrease the risk of developing an allergy. For example, a child who grows up in a house with pets such as cats and dogs, or on a farm, may be less likely to develop an allergic condition. Another statistic shows that children who have suffered certain diseases caused by viruses, such as measles, may have less chance of developing an allergy afterwards. (Of course, these statistics do not take into account the risks of infection from these viruses, which could be more harmful than a mild allergy.)

In general, children from rural areas are slightly less likely to develop an allergy.

Children in city areas with polluted air have a slightly greater chance of developing an allergy.

Hygiene hypothesis

One theory about the increasing number of allergies is an idea called the '**hygiene hypothesis**'. Broadly, it says that children who are brought up in very clean, hygienic, germ-free surroundings become more at risk of developing allergies. This is because their bodies do not encounter germs and natural **allergens** regularly, in small amounts, over the months and years. This means they have less general resistance to fight off health problems.

Linked to the hygiene hypothesis is the idea that people in more developed and industrialized regions are more likely to have allergies than people in more rural areas and less developed countries. One reason might be that people in industrialized regions are more likely to come into contact with a wide range of artificial substances, including food additives, industrial chemicals, pollutants in the air, and mass-produced products, which could act as allergens.

Richer industrialized countries usually have established healthcare systems, with many doctors and hospitals, and more time and money to test people for allergies and record the results. In contrast, people from poorer regions face much greater problems, such as eating enough food to stay alive. In the face of such difficulties, allergies become minor matters that are perhaps not recorded.

Allergies in the nose

Some allergic conditions affect mainly the nose, and cause symptoms similar to those of a common cold. Indeed, some people seem to have a common cold all the time. They sniff with a blocked or runny nose, blow the nose often and cough to clear the throat. They often get headaches, sore throats and earaches. Their eyes may be red and runny. The blocked nose may cause snoring and disturbed sleep.

Perennial allergic rhinitis

These are all symptoms of an allergy called **perennial** (or persistent) allergic **rhinitis**. Rhinitis is when the nose is affected by **inflammation** – swelling, redness, soreness and fluid build up. It occurs mainly in the delicate linings of the air spaces inside the nose, which produce excess **mucus**. It is called perennial rhinitis because it tends to occur all through the year, and so differs from seasonal rhinitis or hay fever (see page 22).

It is estimated that between one in four and one in eight people suffer from perennial allergic rhinitis. It tends to begin in childhood, and it is usually caused by an allergy to tiny floating particles that are breathed in from the air. One of the main **allergens** is the microscopic droppings of the house-**dust mite**. This tiny creature is smaller than the dot on this 'i' and lives among bits of dust, flakes of skin and other debris, in almost any nook or cranny, especially indoors. Its droppings dry out, turn to powder and float in the air. Other allergens for perennial rhinitis are '**dander**' (microflakes of skin, fur or feathers from almost any kind of pet or other animal), plant pollens or micro-spores from moulds and fungi.

People with perennial allergic rhinitis often notice that their symptoms are worse indoors and in places where the allergens collect, such as rooms that are dusty or often used by pets. Some people encounter the allergens regularly due to their work or hobbies, for example, if they involve coming into contact with old hay or straw, mushrooms or fungi, or old or mouldy droppings of cage or aviary birds.

The droppings of the house-dust mite are one of the main allergens that trigger perennial allergic rhinitis.

"Sometimes I just want to cut my nose off and put it in a bowl of cold water to wash it out and stop it itching."

(Anna, a perennial allergic rhinitis sufferer, aged 15)

21

Allergies in the nose

Hay fever and similar allergies

Perennial allergic rhinitis tends to occur all year round. Seasonal allergic rhinitis, as the name suggests, is usually worse at a certain time of year – generally spring or summer, when trees, grass and weeds produce their flowers. These release tiny grains of pollen, which float to other flowers of the same kind, so that seeds can be produced. However, some of the pollen floats into people's noses and throats and lands on their eyes. In some people this causes an **allergic reaction**.

Seasonal allergic rhinitis is often called 'hay fever'. But it is not only triggered by pollen from hay. Almost any pollen can be the cause, coming from flowers, herbs, grasses, bushes or trees. Some people are affected by several types of pollen, over a long period, three months or more. Others are allergic to only one or two types and suffer for just a few days while that particular plant is in flower.

The 'fever' part of the name comes from the similarity of the symptoms to those of a fever or raised temperature, making the sufferer feel generally unwell. They include a runny nose, with sneezing and sniffing and itching; red, sore, runny and itchy eyes; a sore or irritated throat; coughing; and irritated palate (roof of the mouth) and ears. Symptoms may worsen in episodes or attacks, which last about 15–30 minutes, then fade for a time.

In the UK, about one person in six suffers from seasonal allergic rhinitis. About 1 person in 50 consults a doctor each year because of it. And around 1 person in 15 has combined perennial and seasonal rhinitis, where symptoms come and go all year but tend to worsen in the pollen season.

> **❝Sometimes I don't know whether to sing into the mike, or cough or sneeze all over it.❞**
>
> (Nina Persson, vocalist and songwriter with award-winning band, The Cardigans, 1996. She suffers from hay fever.)

Skin allergies

Skin spots, lumps, sores and rashes are very common symptoms of allergy. However, some of these problems are not allergy-based, but caused by chemicals such as household cleaners or strong detergents that irritate and damage the skin. These substances affect everyone, allergic or not. In countries such as the UK and USA, allergy-based skin conditions occur in about one child in seven, and one adult in ten, at some time in their lives.

Urticaria

Urticaria is also called hives. It appears as raised lumps or pale, flat-topped patches called weals or welts, with reddish skin around. The weals are itchy, and they may come and go on different parts of the body. Usually urticaria fades in a few hours. However, it may occur as part of a serious medical condition called **anaphylaxis** (see pages 14–15).

Eczema and dermatitis

This group of skin conditions has many causes and different names. In general, the skin becomes red, inflamed, itchy and sore. Almost any part of the body is vulnerable, although the face, arms and legs are often affected, and particularly the skin creases at joints like the elbow and knee. In babies and children the problem is usually called **atopic** or infantile **eczema**. The skin may become weepy or scabby. In adults the skin is drier and more scaly, and the problem is more likely to be called a skin contact allergy or **dermatitis**.

Urticaria is sometimes known as 'nettle rash' because the poisons in stinging nettles produce a similar effect on the skin.

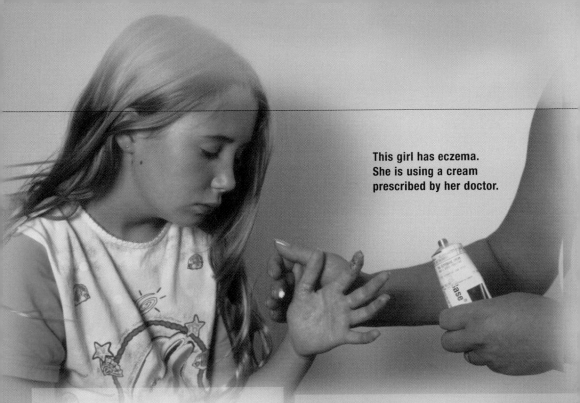

This girl has eczema. She is using a cream prescribed by her doctor.

Causes

The causes of allergic skin conditions vary hugely. It is estimated that food allergy is involved in more than a quarter of eczema-affected babies and children (see page 26). Animal-based **allergens** that float in the air and touch the skin, such as **dust mite** droppings and animal **dander** (see pages 20–21) are also causes. Heat, cold, humidity or bright sunlight can also trigger a skin allergy. Other causes include stress or excitement, exercise that causes flushing and sweating, or some types of fabric, such as wool or nylon.

Chemical allergens

A growing range of products and chemicals can provoke allergic skin conditions. These chemical allergens are found in:

- cosmetics, soaps, perfumes, shampoos, shower gels, hair dyes;
- washing powders and fabric conditioners (often 'biological' or 'enzyme' types);
- detergents, disinfectants, chemical cleaners;
- rubber and latex materials;
- leather (especially if treated and dyed);
- glues and solvents;
- mechanical lubricants such as oils and greases;
- construction materials such as cements, fillers and sealants;
- pure metals, such as nickel, found in bracelets, belt buckles, buttons, fasteners, earrings, piercing studs and other items that come into contact with skin.

Food allergies

About 20 adults out of 100 say they have suffered from a food allergy. However, if these 20 people underwent medical tests, true allergy would be shown in only one or two of them. This is partly explained by other reactions to foods – **intolerance**, **toxicity** and **aversion**. Food intolerance is not a true allergy, but it does trigger processes in the body that result in allergy-like symptoms. They may be due to a lack of a digestive chemical in an individual, or the food may contain the chemical **histamine** (see pages 10–11). In food toxicity, the food contains harmful or poisonous substances that would affect anyone, whether they have an allergy or not. People with food aversion are genuinely convinced that they are allergic to a certain food, but medical tests show no **allergic reaction**.

Symptoms

Symptoms of a genuine food allergy include a widespread skin rash that may itch, also swelling of body parts (noticeable on the face, feet and hands), and problems with breathing, such as wheezing. Longer-term effects may include **eczema** (see previous page), headaches and behaviour changes such as overactivity. Some cases involve abdominal pain, vomiting, diarrhoea and irregular heartbeats (palpitations), but these also occur in food intolerance rather than true allergy. In oral allergy syndrome, the mouth and throat

❝I was lethargic, very tired, with a rash on my forearms so itchy it drove me mad...❞

(Amanda Donohoe [pictured left], British actress, talking about her wheat allergy in 2001)

become red and itchy. In rare but an increasing number of cases, food allergy can threaten a person's life (see pages 40–41).

The main culprits

Almost any food can provoke a reaction. However, six main food ingredients cause nine-tenths of allergy cases in younger people: cow's milk; egg white (albumen); wheat; white fish; peanuts; and soya beans. These foods occur widely, but sometimes they are hidden. For example, milk and eggs are basic cooking ingredients; many breads are baked with wheat (in the form of flour); and soya is found in a huge range of processed and prepared foods.

Other food allergy culprits

- Potatoes
- Cheeses and yoghurts
- Shellfish like mussels, oysters, prawns
- Pork (also ham, bacon, gammon)
- Chicken and other poultry
- Tomatoes, onions and garlic
- Citrus fruits like oranges
- Caffeine (in tea, coffee and cola)
- Soft fruits such as strawberries, peaches, nectarines and kiwis
- Lettuce and artichoke
- Nuts – Brazil nuts, hazelnuts, almonds, pecans, walnuts, cashews, coconuts and pistachios
- Sesame seeds

(For food additives, see page 43.)

Drugs and microbes

About one person in 20 has an **allergic reaction** to a particular drug or medication. This may be in the form of pills, tablets, liquid, droplets, injection, lotion, cream or ointment. The number of people reporting such reactions is about one in eight, but most of these cases are not allergies. They are due to the illness itself, or to taking too much medicine, or to the medicine's side effects.

Drugs can be allergens

The symptoms of a drug allergy usually appear within one or two hours and often involve an itchy rash like **eczema** or **urticaria** (see pages 24–25). More rarely there are longer-term effects several days later, with further skin rashes and problems with internal organs such as the liver and kidneys. In rare cases there is a sudden, serious reaction called **anaphylaxis** (see page 14–15).

Almost any kind of drug or medication might cause an allergy, although most cases are rare. Examples include **antibiotic** drugs such as penicillin, **anaesthetics**, muscle-relaxing drugs used before operations or for painful muscle spasms, various heart drugs and common painkillers such as aspirin and ibuprofen. Some people even become allergic to the antiseptic washes and lotions used to clean wounds and kill germs. Others may be allergic to immunizations (vaccines), such as those given to babies and children against diseases like diphtheria and tetanus.

Medical guidelines urge doctors and pharmacists to check with patients about allergy, whenever a drug is prescribed. People with allergies to medication should mention this to doctors and pharmacists. In most cases patients should wear a Medic-Alert bracelet.

Allergy to infection

People can develop allergies to various **microbes** or germs, such as bacteria and viruses, which cause infectious diseases. The first time the microbes get into the body, they multiply and cause their particular illness in the usual way. But after this first exposure, some people become allergic or **sensitized** to that particular germ. When they encounter that germ again, they suffer an allergic reaction, with symptoms similar to those described above for drug allergy. Examples of infections that people may become allergic to include **glandular fever** and **hepatitis B**.

Bites and stings

A sting from a bee or wasp can be painful and distressing. Some people develop allergies to the poisons or venoms in these stings. They suffer much more pain than a person who does not have an allergy, with redness and swelling, and sometimes a skin rash such as **urticaria**. All of these symptoms last longer than a normal sting. Certain other animals' bites or stings can also provoke an **allergic reaction**. These include ants, gnats, mosquitoes, snakes, scorpions, jellyfish and even the stinging hairs on 'woolly-bear' caterpillars.

Symptoms of the allergic reaction increase the body's normal reaction to the venom. They are usually concentrated at the site of the sting and develop quickly, over minutes. For example, if the bite is on the ankle, then the pain, swelling and

redness may spread into the foot and up the leg to the knee. The affected body part becomes stiff, tense and aching, and movements are painful. There may be severe itching and more widespread swelling, feeling faint and other serious symptoms, which can rapidly develop into a life threatening condition called **anaphylaxis** (see pages 14–15).

Mild to serious stings

Wasp and hornet stings are usually the most serious. Wasps can use their stingers several times, causing more harm than a bee, which can use its sting only once. Effects on the body depend on the sting site and the degree of allergy in the person, and can vary from mild to life-threatening. In the UK each year four or five people die from serious allergic reaction to wasp stings.

A scare for Alan

Alan is 12 and lives in Peekskill, New York state, USA. When Alan was eight, he was enjoying a family summer picnic when he was stung on the wrist — by what, no one saw. Alan cried in shock and pain. The swelling and redness quickly spread up his arm. His parents took him to the nearest medical centre. Alan was having an allergic reaction to the sting. The allergic reaction was treated and gradually faded. Alan and his parents received valuable advice about avoiding such problems in the future, and about first aid in case of anaphylaxis.

Diagnosis and support

Is it an allergy?

Most people who think they may have an allergy should visit their doctor. The doctor asks various questions about the symptoms, when they happen, for how long and what appears to cause them in order to determine what the **allergen** could be. It helps if the person has already kept notes about when **allergic reactions** occur. Some people keep a 'food diary', recording everything they eat, or a 'place diary' of rooms and other sites visited, noting any allergic reactions they may have. Follow-up medical tests, either at a health centre or at a specialist allergy clinic, may identify the allergen more precisely.

Skin prick test

Skin prick tests involve putting several droplets of fluid, each containing an allergen, in rows on to the skin, usually on the forearm. The skin under each droplet is pricked with a small lancet so that the

allergen can enter the body. An allergic reaction shows as a small, swollen, pale, raised, itchy area at the prick site. It develops within 15–20 minutes, then gradually fades. The bigger the affected area, the greater the reaction.

Patch and blood tests

In the patch test, small discs coated with potential allergens are taped on to the skin, usually for 48 hours. The skin areas are studied for reactions such as **eczema** or **dermatitis**. Blood samples may also be taken and analyzed in the laboratory. If a person has

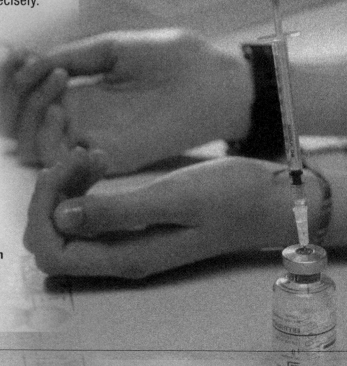

Patch tests on the skin can even reveal reactions to allergens that normally cause symptoms elsewhere, such as in the nose.

reacted to the allergens before, there will be **antibodies** against them in the blood (see pages 10–11).

Challenge tests

In a challenge test, the person is directly exposed to a suspected allergen under strict medical conditions. In the case of food allergy, the person may not be told that the suspected food is in a meal or capsule. This helps to screen out non-allergic reactions such as food **aversion** (see pages 26–27).

Maureen's 'allergy'

Maureen lives in Brisbane, Australia. When she was 14, she suffered stomach pains, which came on after some meals. Maureen's older brother, Jim, had severe **asthma**, and her parents knew that allergies run in families. They thought Maureen might have a food allergy. Over several weeks Maureen kept a food diary of exactly what she ate. The stomach pains varied but there was no clear link with a particular food. Finally Maureen went to her family doctor. After a few tests the problem was identified as a stomach ulcer. Maureen discovered that stomach pain, on its own, is rarely a symptom of food allergy.

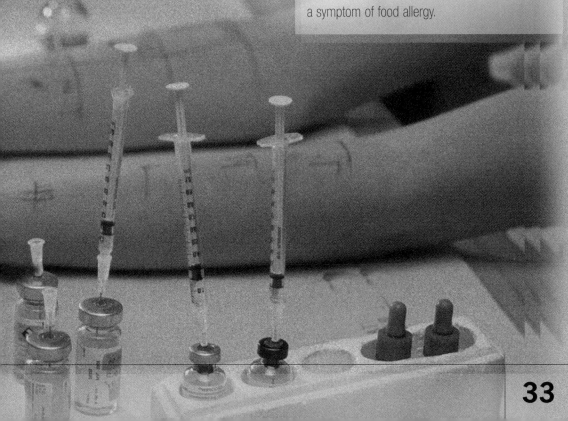

Diagnosis and support

Tackling an allergy

For many health problems such as a common cold or sprained wrist, people usually suffer for a while, then get better. However, an allergy may have far-reaching and long-lasting effects on everyday life. Medical treatments can help greatly, by lessening the symptoms and allowing the patient greater freedom. But people with allergies can also help themselves. By taking responsibility for their condition and having a positive attitude, rather than trying to ignore symptoms, they can keep their allergy under control.

People who can help

There are many professionals in the healthcare system who can offer advice about coping with an allergy. They include the family doctor or GP, health centre nurses and advisors, hospital doctors and consultants, and allergy specialists, who are usually based at allergy clinics. Dietitians can offer valuable advice for food allergies and dermatologists are specially trained to treat skin allergies. There is also a huge range of complementary practitioners (see pages 46–47). In addition, there are many self-help

groups run by people with allergies. They share their experiences and knowledge, and pass on useful advice and practical tips to other people with allergies.

Support from family and friends

Family and friends of a person with an allergy have an important role to play. Their understanding, tolerance and patience can help the person to cope well, rather than feeling a burden on others. People with allergies may have times when they feel picked on or singled out because of their condition. For example, they may not want to go outside on a sunny summer day because they know in a few minutes they will be sneezing with itchy eyes from hay fever. But their friends and family might misinterpret this as being 'wimpy' or not interested in exercise or sport. Sometimes people with allergies become angry or depressed. Younger children with an allergy may not understand their condition. They often feel annoyed or left out because they cannot eat certain foods, or keep pets, or play outside, as their friends do.

Family and friends can give support and encouragement at these times. At the same time, they can watch for signs that the sufferer is becoming obsessed or dominated by the allergy, and letting it affect daily life unduly.

'Why me?' is a common question for people with long-term health problems. But dwelling on the negative side can make things feel worse.

Living with allergy

Coping with an allergy in daily life can be seen as a balancing act. On one side is the need to be aware of the problem, take precautions and avoid the **allergen** as much as possible. This reduces symptoms, suffering, the need for medication and the possible risk of serious **allergic reaction**. On the other side is the problem of taking so much care and so many precautions that everyday life becomes

unreasonably restricted, with constant worry and fear of being exposed to the allergen.

Many people with allergies develop the habit of adding the word 'allergy' to any lists, plans or arrangements they make. A day in the country, eating out at a friend's house, a holiday, a shopping trip for foods or household goods could all lead to allergen exposure. It is important to anticipate if exposure is likely, and to take precautions, such as having antihistamine medication available.

Allergies at home

Home is a place where people spend a lot of time – and also where they have greatest control over their surroundings. For many types of allergy, there are practical precautions that can be carried out at home, to avoid exposure to allergens. For example, with **perennial rhinitis** caused by allergy to **dust mite** droppings, it is important to take extra care when cleaning, to remove dust from nooks and crannies.

People with food allergies can help themselves by checking labels to make sure that possible allergens are not contained in the foods they buy.

A vacuum cleaner with an allergen filter is more effective than an ordinary vacuum cleaner. Dust-proof enclosed covers on mattresses, duvets, pillows and cushions also reduce the risk. Air and dust filters can also be useful.

For a food allergy, it is important to check all food items on shelves, in cupboards, larders and freezers, for the allergenic food or ingredient. When buying foods, all food packages and labels should be checked to make sure the allergen is not contained in any of the products. Labelling regulations are gradually improving in this respect. For example, in most countries it must be clearly stated if a food may contain nuts or even traces of nuts.

There are similar practical tips for other allergies. Family members and friends can help by appreciating the problems of the person with the allergy, suggesting ideas, and keeping a lookout for times when exposure to the allergen may occur.

❝Let the person control the allergy – not the other way around.❞

(Advice for coping with an allergy in daily life)

Living with allergy

Away from home

For many people with allergies, there are fewer worries about being at home, compared to being out and about, where they have less control over the environment. Going to school, college, the workplace or even on holiday – these are all places where a person might come into contact with possible allergens.

Taking simple precautions such as remembering to pack allergy medication makes sure that a holiday is safe, comfortable ... and fun!

Planning ahead

Before going out and about, it helps to think ahead and make plans to minimize exposure to allergens. For example, when eating out at a restaurant or cafe, it is advised to telephone ahead to discuss a food allergy with the chef. With enough warning, the staff can offer alternative dishes. This avoids the problem of turning up for the meal to find that choosing a dish is difficult, which may spoil an otherwise pleasant experience.

For any allergy, planning ahead helps to avoid situations where the sufferer is put in an awkward position, requiring 'special treatment'. This draws unwanted attention to the allergy. It may make the person with the allergy feel guilty or at fault. For most types of allergies, there are lists of protective measures, precautions and useful equipment that can help to reduce allergen exposure. This applies especially to places where people spend much time, such as classrooms or workplaces. Schools, colleges and employers usually have legal duties to take into account more serious allergies, although the regulations differ from region to region. For example, a child who suffers severe hay fever can avoid exposure to pollen by being allowed to stay indoors at school during the main hay fever season. A person with a food allergy can have this taken into account when meals are prepared at school or work – in the same way as for people with other dietary requirements, such as those with diabetes.

Kelly's plate of food

Kelly is eight years old and lives in Toronto, Canada. Kelly is allergic to wheat. When she was younger, Kelly's allergy used to cause her great upset at school. The staff always tried to disguise the fact that her meals were specially prepared, so they could not understand why Kelly got upset. It turned out that it was not the food that caused the problem, but the plate. The staff had used a different colour of plate for Kelly, to identify her meal, but she did not like being seen as 'different' from her friends.

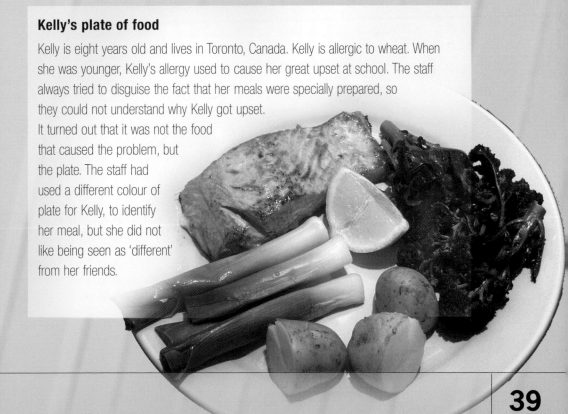

Living with allergy

Kirsty's story

On Kirsty's tenth birthday, she went ten-pin bowling with some girlfriends in Edinburgh, Scotland. The girls were having a great time. After the first game they had a break for snacks and drinks. Kirsty was very excited, with the bowling and her birthday. She forgot what she should always do, and what she'd been doing for years – to check that her food contained no nuts or nut traces of any kind.

When Kirsty was two, just after eating peanut butter on toast, she was very ill and could not breathe properly. Her parents rushed her to hospital. Soon afterwards, tests showed that Kirsty had an allergy to some nuts. Since then, Kirsty's parents always avoided giving her any nuts – even tiny traces such as nut oils or flavourings. Sometimes it meant having special meals, but they had all got used to it. Kirsty often checked her own snacks and meals, read food labels, and asked if there were any nuts in any food she was given. But, on her birthday, she forgot. After eating an ice cream she felt faint and breathless, and slumped in the chair. The bowling centre had a trained first-aider who called an ambulance. In the ambulance, Kirsty was given an adrenaline injection (adrenaline increases heart rate and blood pressure, and helps open up the airways, making it easier to breathe).

Medical specialists called allergists can provide useful advice to prevent an allergy from interfering with daily life.

At hospital, Kirsty recovered well. A few days later, Kirsty visited her own doctor with her parents for a check-up. The doctor arranged for new tests. The tests showed exactly what she was allergic to, and how strongly. The doctor also arranged for her to see an allergy specialist the following week. Kirsty said the specialist was 'brilliant'. She told Kirsty about the many kinds of medicines to help an allergy, and how new ones were always on the market. She advised Kirsty to wear a special bracelet or necklace to warn others about her allergy, and to carry a card with information about what to do in an emergency. Best of all, the allergist gave Kirsty lots of useful tips about how to check foods and meals for nuts, and how to remember to do this every day – even on birthdays!

Prevention and treatment

Treating symptoms

There is a vast range of products and preparations available, which can reduce the symptoms of an **allergic reaction** and ease suffering. They include eye drops, soothing skin creams and nasal sprays.

Pharmacists, doctors, allergy specialists or self-help groups can provide a lot of useful advice.

Substances called **emollients** are particularly useful for allergies that affect the skin, such as forms of **eczema** or **dermatitis**. These conditions can be distressing for babies and young children, who do not understand what is happening and why they should not scratch such an annoying itch. Emollients soften, moisturize and soothe the skin. They can be in the form of creams, ointments, oils and lotions, and can be spread on the skin or added to bath water.

Allergy eye drops can help to soothe red, itchy eyes and also wash away the allergen.

Additional advice for preventing and treating eczema or dermatitis includes:

- Avoid soaps, gels and shampoos. Even some '**hypoallergenic**' types (meaning they contain very low amounts of possible allergens) can cause problems. People with eczema or dermatitis should try different types of hypoallergenic products to find out which ones work best.
- Pat rather than rub the skin dry.
- Wear loose-fitting clothes with cotton next to the skin.
- As far as possible, avoid strong emotions, worry and stress. These can worsen many allergic conditions, especially eczema or dermatitis.

Food additives

Numerous substances added to foods can cause allergic reactions or food **intolerance** (see page 26). These substances are more common in processed, pre-prepared, packaged and take-away foods. Additives used in the European Community are referred to as 'E numbers'. The range of food additives used are extremely varied. Some are natural substances, others are artificial chemicals. There is no medically recognized 'allergy to all E numbers'.

Brightly coloured sweets usually contain food dyes or colourings.

E numbers that can cause allergic reactions

- Sulphites (containing sulphur, E220–227), which are used as preservatives and to prevent discolouring.
- Benzoic acids (E210–219) and parabens, which prevent **microbes** spoiling or rotting foods and are also found in creams, ointments and other medications.
- Antioxidants such as BHA (E320), BHT (E321), which prevent oils and fats turning rancid, or bad.
- Flavourings such as the 'slimming sweetener' aspartame and 'flavour enhancer' monosodium glutamate (MSG, E620).
- Colourings including 'azo dyes' such as tartrazine (E102), and sunset yellow (E110).

Prevention and treatment

Medications

Medications used to treat allergies vary from mild, over-the-counter versions, to powerful prescription drugs. Since allergies are so varied, a drug that works for one sufferer may not suit another, even for the same allergy. Anyone with an allergy should consult a healthcare professional before using a particular treatment. Doctors and pharmacists advise on the range of drugs available, so that a person with an allergy can test various products to find out the most effective one in his or her case.

Antihistamines

Antihistamines reduce the effect of **histamine**, the main body chemical that causes **allergic reaction**. Antihistamines decrease itching and may help other symptoms. They are especially useful for hay fever and other forms of **rhinitis**, and for some skin conditions. There are dozens of different types available. Many come in pill, tablet or liquid form, while some are applied directly to the affected area as ointments or droplets. Certain types work very quickly but only for a short time, while 'all-day' versions act for many hours.

Steroids

Steroid (corticosteroid) drugs prevent or reduce swelling, congestion, redness and other features of **inflammation**. 'Preventers' are taken regularly in low doses to prevent symptoms. 'Relievers' are used

if symptoms are likely or begin. Steroids may be inhaled as a nasal spray, taken as eye drops (under medical supervision), or as pills (also under medical supervision).

other rhinitis sufferers. However they should only be used for a short time. If used for longer periods, the congestion tends to comes back more severely.

Decongestants

Decongestant nasal sprays or tablets can also be helpful, especially for hay fever and

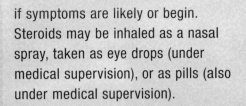

Warning

For any drug, it is important to read the information on the package and leaflet inside. Some drugs, including certain antihistamines, cause side effects such as drowsiness or sleepiness. For this reason, they are not recommended for people who need to be alert, as when driving, operating machinery or taking examinations. Steroids, in particular, should be taken only under strict medical supervision and according to the instructions.

Prevention and treatment

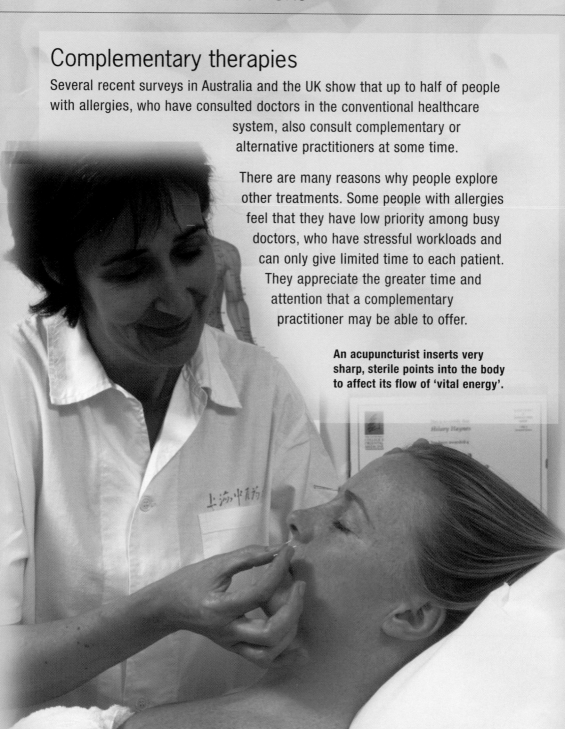

Complementary therapies

Several recent surveys in Australia and the UK show that up to half of people with allergies, who have consulted doctors in the conventional healthcare system, also consult complementary or alternative practitioners at some time.

There are many reasons why people explore other treatments. Some people with allergies feel that they have low priority among busy doctors, who have stressful workloads and can only give limited time to each patient. They appreciate the greater time and attention that a complementary practitioner may be able to offer.

An acupuncturist inserts very sharp, sterile points into the body to affect its flow of 'vital energy'.

They may also feel they are being understood and treated as a whole person, rather than simply being offered medical drugs for specific symptoms. Some people believe that complementary treatments or alternative therapies could be safer and more 'natural', with fewer side effects than conventional medicines. Some explore complementary methods for the reason that the name suggests – to complement, or add to, their other treatments.

Range of complementary therapies

Some of the better-known therapies for allergies include herbal and Bach flower remedies, homeopathy and acupuncture. In acupuncture, sharp needles are placed into the body at certain points, with the aim of affecting the flow of what practitioners call chi or 'vital energy' through the body. For a food allergy, the needle points are chosen to direct energy to the stomach and intestines in the lower body, so the energy is able to overcome the allergic reaction.

Certain people suffer more from their allergies when they are under stress or worried. They find that relaxation techniques such as yoga and hypnotherapy may help. For others, a person called a clinical ecologist considers many aspects of the environment and surroundings, at home and work and play, including water, air, food, housing, daily habits and levels of pollution, to discover causes or **triggers** of the allergy.

Success rates

The response of individual patients to these therapies is difficult to predict. Also scientific studies show that success rates of many therapies are often no greater than would be expected by chance. However, it is accepted that most of these techniques have helped some allergy sufferers. People who consider trying these types of treatments are advised to make contact with a practitioner through their own doctor or an established national organization (see pages 52–53).

Can allergy be cured?

In the same way that an allergy can develop at almost any age, it can also fade at any time. The medical reasons for this are unclear. But doctors often reassure patients that, for common allergies such as **eczema** and hay fever, 'age is the best cure'. Statistics show that many babies and children gradually lose their allergies through their teenage years or twenties. For every ten babies and toddlers who develop eczema, about five will no longer suffer from it by six years of age, and another four will be free of it ten years later. Some 'cures' claimed by allergy treatments may well result from this natural tendency for people to lose allergy with age.

Desensitization

Desensitization is when the body is exposed to gradually increasing amounts of **allergen**. This is usually given by injection at regular intervals, such as each week. The complete course lasts three years or more. The technique tends to work best for a person sensitive to only one allergen, such as a single type of plant pollen. It requires strict medical supervision due to the small risk of a severe **allergic reaction** after an injection. Patients attend a specialist clinic for injections, and wait for one hour afterwards, until the risk period for severe reaction has passed. Desensitization is also known as desensitization **immunotherapy**, allergen-specific immunotherapy (SIT), or allergy injections, 'shots' or 'jabs'.

Desensitization is more popular with doctors in some countries than others. It has most success against breathed-in allergens, such as pollen, and also against venoms such as bee and wasp stings. However it requires regular attendance by the patient for injections over a long period, and it can be costly. There is no guarantee of success. Surveys show that desensitization works well, or partly, in many cases.

James is 'cured'

James, aged 16, lived in Sheffield, UK and had suffered from hay fever ever since he was five years old. When he was ten, his family moved to a village near Grimsby, on the coast. At the time of the move, his parents worried greatly that James' hay fever would worsen. In fact, it almost disappeared. The local doctor suggested that James was probably allergic to pollen from city park trees, which did not grow near his new home. Also winds tended to blow in from the sea, and so carried less pollen of all kinds.

Some allergy sufferers find that the cleaner air of coastal regions can reduce their symptoms.

Can allergy be cured?

Hopes for the future

Many areas of research aim to make allergies less of a problem. For example, millions of allergy sufferers use medication as the most convenient form of control. So drug companies continue to develop new antihistamines, **steroids** and other medical drugs, which work better and have fewer side effects.

The main progress in allergy research is towards more effective and safer medications. This immunologist is testing new treatments on human tissue. She is looking for inflamed cells – a sign of an allergic reaction.

Various public health measures could help allergy sufferers. These include banning smoking and reducing heating in public places such as shopping malls, providing clearer warnings of possible **allergens** on packaging, especially for foods and skin products, and planting more low-allergy grasses, flowers and trees in parks, gardens and farms. However, such measures often lose out to other demands for safeguarding the public, such as improving road safety.

SLIT

A newer form of desensitization (see page 48) is SLIT, sub-lingual **immunotherapy**. Increasing amounts of the allergen are given daily as droplets under the tongue. This may do away with the need to attend specialist clinics for injections and reduce the risk of severe allergic reaction. Early results have been encouraging, but there are still many trials and safety tests to pass before it can become a widely adopted treatment.

Modern living

Basic research continues into links between allergies and food, air, water, homes, pollution, lifestyle, climate change and almost every other aspect of modern life. Better understanding of allergies may allow parents to reduce the risks of their children developing them, for example, by avoiding certain foods in the first year of life. Supporters of the '**hygiene hypothesis**' (explained on page 19) suggest that exposure to a carefully tested mix of **microbes** and common allergens, early in life, may reduce the general risk of developing an allergy later. This could work in the same way as the vaccines or immunizations given as injections against diseases such as polio, measles, mumps and rubella (German measles).

Genetic research

It may also be possible to use our fast-growing base of genetic information and new technologies to fight allergies. If the precise make-up of common allergens is worked out, this could lead to vaccines against them. Or plants and even animals might be genetically modified, so they do not produce allergens – either when alive or when eaten as foods. However, there does not seem to be a 'magic bullet' drug or wonder cure method for allergies in the near future.

Information and advice

Many organizations offer advice about allergies and have helplines giving further information.

Contacts in the UK

Allergy UK
Deepdene House, 30 Bellegrove Road, Welling, Kent DA16 3PY
Tel: 020 8303 8525
Helpline: 020 8303 8583 (Monday – Friday 9 a.m.–9 p.m.; and Saturday 9 a.m.–1 p.m.)
Email: info@allergyuk.org
Website: www.allergyfoundation.com/
The UK's national medical allergy charity, established to increase understanding and awareness of allergy, provide information, advice and support on most allergies and chemical sensitivities, help people manage their allergies, raise funds for allergy research and provide training in allergy for health care professionals.

Anaphylaxis Campaign
Anaphylaxis helpline: 01252 542029
Website: www.anaphylaxis.org.uk/
An independent charity guided by leading UK allergists providing information for those affected by allergies, news, food alerts, special pages for young people with allergies and educational products.

National Eczema Society
Hill House, Highgate Hill, London N19 5NA
Tel: 020 7281 3553
Eczema information and helpline: 0870 241 3604 (Monday – Friday 9 a.m.–5 p.m.)
Website: www.eczema.org/
One of the most established organizations worldwide dedicated to the needs of people with eczema, dermatitis and sensitive skin.

It provides a comprehensive information and advice service, an extensive network of local contacts and support, funds for research and a campaigning voice on behalf of people with eczema.

Contacts in the USA

Food Allergy & Anaphylaxis Network (US HQ)
10400 Eaton Place, Suite 107, Fairfax, VA 22030-2208
Tel: 800-929-4040
Website: www.foodallergy.org/
The Food Allergy & Anaphylaxis Network (FAAN) was established in 1991 to be a world leader in food allergy and anaphylaxis awareness, and the issues surrounding this condition.

Contacts in Australia

FACTS Australia (Food Anaphylactic Children Training and Support Association)
21 Robinson Close, Hornsby Heights, NSW 2077
Tel: 1300 728 000
A non-profit organization whose members provide their skills, time and energy on a voluntary basis to help families with food anaphylactic children.

Australasian Society of Clinical Immunology and Allergy (ASCIA)
PO Box 450, Balgowlah, NSW 2093
Tel: 0425 216 402
Website: www.allergy.org.au/aer/infobulletins/index.htm
ASCIA education resources are dedicated to informing the community on allergy, asthma and immunology issues. They provide up-to-date and reliable information to enable

patients and their doctors to make informed choices about management for allergy, asthma and immune diseases.

Contacts in New Zealand

Allergy New Zealand
PO Box 56-117, Dominion Road, Auckland
Allergy Info Line: 09-303 2024
Toll Free: 0800 34 0800
Website: www.allergy.org.nz/
Allergy New Zealand aims to improve the quality of life for people with allergies and their families, through support, education and information.

Websites

All Allergy
http://allallergy.net/
The gateway to asthma, allergy and intolerance information on the Internet – launched to respond to the need for rapid access, including articles, pharmaceuticals, occupational information, clinics and centres, support groups, mailing lists, books, newsletters, journals, news and much, much more, searchable by country.

Food Allergy and Anaphylaxis Alliance
www.foodallergyalliance.org
An international group of allergy charities providing international links on the worldwide web.

Further reading

Allergies (Health Matters) by Carol Baldwin; Heinemann Library, 2002

Allergies (My Health) by Alvin Silverstein, Virginia Silverstein, Laura Silverstein Nunn; Franklin Watts Inc., 1999

Allergies (Millbrook Medical Library) by Wendy Moragne; Twenty-first Century Books, 1999

Allergies (21st Century Health & Wellness) by Edward Edelson; Chelsea House, Revised edition 1999

Allergies (Rookie Read-About Health) by Sharon Gordon; Children's Press, 2003

Allergies and Hay Fever – The British Medical Association Family Doctor Guide by Dr Robert J. Davies; Dorling Kindersley, 1999

Coping With Eczema by Robert Youngson; Sheldon Press, 1995

Hay Fever: The Complete Guide by Jonathan Brostoff, Linda Gamlin; Inner Traditions International Ltd, 2002

Glossary

allergen
a substance that causes an allergic reaction

allergic reaction
when a person's body reacts to a normally harmless substance, an allergen, causing effects such as swelling, redness, itching and fluid build-up in various areas

anaesthetics
substances that lessen or remove feelings and sensations, including touch and pain

anaphylaxis
a sudden and severe allergic reaction that may interfere with breathing and cause heart problems, and may threaten life. Anaphylaxis needs emergency expert medical treatment.

antibiotics
medical drugs that kill or disable the types of germs called bacteria

antibodies
substances made by the body to kill or damage invading germs or other harmful items; in allergy, antibodies are made against normally harmless substances such as plant pollen

asthma
an allergy-based condition which usually causes wheezing and difficulty in breathing

atopic
a tendency to develop allergic conditions, in particular those such as eczema, asthma and hay fever, especially when young

aversion
a dislike of something

dander
tiny particles of skin, fur, feathers or other substances from animals

decongestant
a substance that lessens congestion, the build-up of fluids and mucus in or on a body part, such as when the nose is blocked

dermatitis
a skin condition usually caused by an allergy, where patches of skin become reddened, sore and itchy, and dry or scaly, or moist and 'weeping' (often also called eczema)

dust mites
tiny eight-legged creatures that live in house dust, whose powdered droppings cause allergic reactions in some people

eczema
a skin condition usually caused by an allergy, where patches of skin become reddened, sore and itchy, and dry or scaly, or moist and 'weeping' (often also called dermatitis)

emollient
a substance that softens and soothes the skin

genes
instructions for how the body develops and carries out life processes, which are in the form of the chemical DNA

glandular fever
an infection causing fever, headache, sore throat and swollen glands, mainly in the neck, but also in the armpits and groin. It is sometimes accompanied by a skin rash.

hepatitis B
an infection of the liver causing weakness, digestive problems, yellowing of the skin, fever, appetite loss, nausea and other symptoms

histamine
a body chemical, which causes symptoms of an allergy such as swelling, redness, itching and fluid build-up in the affected parts

hygiene hypothesis
a theory about why allergies develop in certain people, based on the idea that the body's surroundings are 'too clean' and the body does not encounter enough germs and other problems

hypoallergenic
containing only very small amounts of possible allergens

immune system
the body's own self-defence system, which fights infection and provides resistance to disease

immunotherapy
medical treatment that involves the immune system

inflammation
redness, swelling, soreness, build-up of fluid, pain and perhaps itching of a body part, usually due to infection, injury or an allergic reaction

intolerance
being unable to deal with or cope with something, either in behaviour, or in the body's processes

mast cells
microscopic body cells that are part of the immune system, and which release the body chemical histamine during an allergic reaction

microbe
a microscopic living thing. Microbes include harmful types of germs such as bacteria and viruses.

mucus
slimy fluid produced by the body, especially by the inner linings of the nose, mouth, throat, airways, lungs, gullet, stomach and intestines

perennial
occurring or being present more or less all the time, rather than now and again or seasonally

rhinitis
inflammation, redness, soreness and fluid build-up in the nose and nasal passages, usually in their linings. It causes sneezing, itching, blockage or dripping, and general irritation.

sensitization
the period after a person has first been exposed to an allergen, during which their immune system 'learns' to recognize the substance

steroid
medication used to prevent or reduce swelling, congestion, redness and other features of inflammation

toxicity
when a substance is toxic (poisonous or harmful in some way)

trigger
a substance or condition that begins or sets off a process, such as plant pollen that triggers an allergic reaction in the eyes and nose during hay fever

tuberculosis
a serious infection that causes fever, weakness, coughing and breathing problems and other symptoms

urticaria
a skin condition with pale, flat-topped, red-edged lumps or weals that itch or sting. It can be caused by stinging nettles or other stinging or poisonous plants or animals, or by an allergic reaction.

Index

Titles in the *Need to Know* series include:

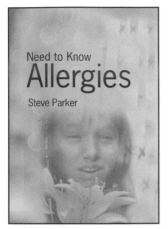

Need to Know
Allergies
Steve Parker

Hardback   0 431 09760 7

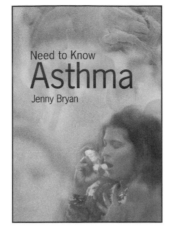

Need to Know
Asthma
Jenny Bryan

Hardback   0 431 09761 5

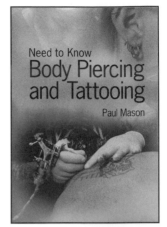

Need to Know
Body Piercing and Tattooing
Paul Mason

Hardback   0 431 09818 2

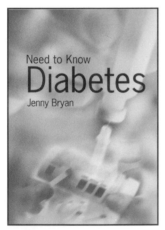

Need to Know
Diabetes
Jenny Bryan

Hardback   0 431 09762 3

Need to Know
Eating Disorders
Caroline Warbrick

Hardback   0 431 09799 2

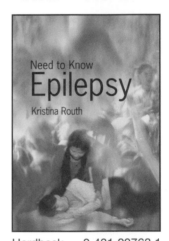

Need to Know
Epilepsy
Kristina Routh

Hardback   0 431 09763 1

Need to Know
Multiple Sclerosis
Alexander Burnfield

Hardback   0 431 09764 X

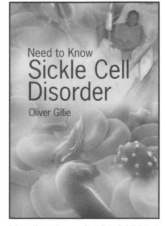

Need to Know
Sickle Cell Disorder
Oliver Gillie

Hardback   0 431 09765 8

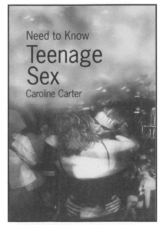

Need to Know
Teenage Sex
Caroline Carter

Hardback   0 431 09821 2

Find out about the other titles in this series on our website www.heinemann.co.uk/library